"Charles Eastman is the first major Indian author to write Indian history from the Indian perspective."
  —Raymond Wilson, author of *Ohiyesa: Charles Eastman, Santee Sioux*, and editor of *Native Americans in the Twentieth Century*

ABOUT THIS BOOK

"[This book] is very effectively edited by Michael Fitzgerald for today's young children of all races and ethnic backgrounds. . . . This version highlights the important points in Ohiyesa's life in the wilderness, as well as the challenging hardships and the lessons he was taught in preparation for life as a warrior and hunter. All of the telling is complemented by Heidi Rasch's exciting, colorful, and authentic illustrations of the Dakota people and of nature that was so integral to Indian life. . . . Charles Eastman has long been a hero and role model to me. We are both mixed-blood Sioux; he a Santee Dakota and me an Oglala Lakota."
  —Charles Trimble, former Executive Director of the National Congress of American Indians, and author of *Iyeska*

"Michael Fitzgerald has captured the extraordinary values in a Dakota Sioux upbringing through interpreting Charles Eastman's writing of his childhood as the freest in the world. Educators and parents who wish to teach critical lessons on life and survival to their young will find this book valuable as a readiness model for living."
  —Vivian Arviso Deloria, former Executive Director of Education for the Navajo Nation and Chairperson of the Navajo Nation Women's Commission

ABOUT THE EDITOR

"My son, Michael Fitzgerald, has been a member of my family and the Crow tribe for over twenty years. Michael has helped to preserve the spiritual traditions of the Crow Sun Dance and he has helped to show us the wisdom of the old-timers."
  —Thomas Yellowtail, Crow medicine man and Sun Dance chief

CHARLES EASTMAN (OHIYESA)
INDIAN BOYHOOD
THE TRUE STORY OF A SIOUX UPBRINGING

EDITED AND ADAPTED BY
MICHAEL OREN FITZGERALD

ILLUSTRATED BY HEIDI M. RASCH

FOREWORD BY CHARLES TRIMBLE

❖Wisdom Tales❖

To my family ~ HMR

Indian Boyhood:
The True Story of a Sioux Upbringing
©Wisdom Tales, 2016

Book design by Stephen Williams

Wisdom Tales is an imprint of World Wisdom, Inc.

Library of Congress Cataloging-in-Publication Data

Names: Eastman, Charles A., 1858-1939 | Fitzgerald, Michael Oren, 1949-
editor. | Rasch, Heidi M., illustrator.
Title: Indian boyhood : the true story of a Sioux upbringing / by Charles
Eastman (Ohiyesa) ; edited and adapted by Michael Oren Fitzgerald ;
illustrated by Heidi M. Rasch ; foreword by Charles Trimble.
Description: Bloomington, IN : Wisdom Tales, [2016] | Includes
bibliographical references.
Identifiers: LCCN 2015047423 (print) | LCCN 2015048369 (ebook) | ISBN
9781937786564 (casebound : alk. paper) | ISBN 9781937786571 (epub)
Subjects: LCSH: Eastman, Charles Alexander, 1858-1939--Childhood and
youth--Juvenile literature. | Santee Indians--Social life and
customs--Juvenile literature. | Santee Indians--Biography--Juvenile literature.
Classification: LCC E99.S22 E184 (print) | LCC E99.S22 (ebook) | DDC
978.3004/9752440092--dc23
LC record available at http://lccn.loc.gov/2015047423

Printed in China on acid-free paper

Production Date: January 2016,
Plant & Location: Printed by 1010 Printing International Ltd.,
Job Batch #: TT16010081

For information address Wisdom Tales,
P.O. Box 2682, Bloomington, Indiana 47402-2682
www.wisdomtalespress.com

FOREWORD

Charles Alexander Eastman was born into the traditional world of the Dakota (Sioux). He was the last of five children born to the union of Mary Nancy Eastman, a mixed-blood Dakota woman, and Many Lightnings, a full-blood Santee Dakota man. His mother died soon after his birth; but on her deathbed she gave the child to his paternal grandmother to rear as her own. Charles was given the name Hakadah, "the Pitiful Last," denoting his pathetic entry to the family—a motherless newborn with slim chances of survival. He was later given the name Ohiyesa, "the Victor," a name that would prove prophetic in Eastman's amazing life.

In his earliest years, his world was transformed by the growing presence of immigrant peoples in Sioux Country, and by the inevitable conflict between the Native and the European cultures. In the so-called Indian Uprising of 1862 the Dakota people rebelled against white incursions onto their lands and the government's withholding of treaty-guaranteed rations that left them starving. Ohiyesa's extended family fled to Canada to escape the U.S. Army, which was hell-bent on brutal vengeance, and there in the isolation of northern wilderness he spent his youth, coming of age immersed in traditional Dakota lifeways.

This story is told in Eastman's first book, *Indian Boyhood*. Published in 1902, the book remains a classic in literature about Native America and a treasure for the preservation of a traditional culture that Indian people today strive to emulate and to restore in the modern world.

That very same story is presented in this book that carries the same title as the original *Indian Boyhood*. It is very effectively edited by Michael Fitzgerald for today's young children of all races and ethnic backgrounds, albeit in the English language. This version highlights the important points in Ohiyesa's life in the wilderness, as well as the challenging hardships and the lessons he was taught in preparation for life as a warrior and hunter. All of the telling is complemented by Heidi Rasch's exciting, colorful, and authentic illustrations of the Dakota people and of nature that was so integral to Indian life.

It is my hope that all youngsters who will be engrossed in this book will be inspired to read the original version of *Indian Boyhood*, as well as the other great books on Indian life and culture by Charles Eastman. And it is my hope that parents, some of whom might be called upon to read this book to younger children who are not yet able to read, will also be so inspired.

Charles Eastman has long been a hero and role model to me. We are both mixed-blood Sioux; he a Santee Dakota and me an Oglala Lakota. He came into the world as Hakadah, "the Pitiful Last," and in his earliest years had experienced bitter pain and hardship. But when the time came to put behind him the freedom of life in the wilderness and enter the alien world of the whiteman, he held no resentment, no bitterness: instead, he seized the opportunities, embraced the challenges, and lived a long full life as a physician, an authority on Indian affairs, a lecturer, and an activist for America to keep its treaty promises for a better life for all Indian tribes and peoples.

He was, after all, Ohiyesa, the victor.

—Charles Trimble

EDITOR'S PREFACE

Charles Eastman (1858-1939), Santee Dakota, is widely considered to be the preeminent American Indian spokesperson of the early twentieth century. Yet, Eastman is unknown to most people, even though he was the main character in the HBO film, *Bury My Heart at Wounded Knee*. This book's goal is to introduce young children to this great American and spark a lifelong interest in studying other cultures, particularly the American Indian world. I believe Eastman's insights can help each of us better understand our own modern civilization.

This is the story of Charles Eastman's boyhood from 1858 until 1873, during which time he was raised in the traditional nomadic life of his Dakota Sioux people.[1] The text is adapted directly from the first of Eastman's eleven books, *Indian Boyhood*, published in 1902. It may be helpful to have additional information about the editing process. Several pages are direct quotes. For example, the first page presents the opening paragraph of *Indian Boyhood*: "What boy would not be an Indian for a while when he thinks of the freest life in the world? This life was mine. Every day there was a real hunt. There was real game."

However, it was necessary to simplify the text in many places for younger readers. For example, Eastman often refers to himself in the third person, including his boyhood Indian name, Hakadah. He writes, "Sometimes, when Hakadah wakened too early in the morning, she would sing to him something like the following lullaby: …" My adaptation uses first person pronouns to refer to Eastman and shortens the text, "Sometimes, when I wakened too early, my grandmother would sing me a lullaby."

This is Eastman's closing paragraph in *Indian Boyhood*: "Late in the fall we reached the citizen settlement at Flandreau, South Dakota, where my father and some others dwelt among the whites. Here my wild life came to an end, and my school days began." This is my adaptation on the final page: "Late in the fall we reached the town where my father and some others lived. Here my wild life came to an end, and my school days began."

I close the book by repeating the important statement Eastman used to begin *Indian Boyhood*: "Yet, I repeat, what boy would not be an Indian for a while when he thinks of the freest life in the world?" These adaptations are necessary to accurately convey Eastman's thoughts to young readers.

This work is not for profit. All author and illustrator royalties will be donated to various American Indian causes. I will be profoundly satisfied with this project if it encourages some children to learn more about Charles Eastman and the First Peoples on our continent.

—Michael Fitzgerald
Bloomington, Indiana

1. The term "Sioux" is used in this book because Eastman included it in his writings. It refers to the political structure of his people at the time of their contact with Europeans and Euro-Americans. The Lakota, Nakota, and Dakota Nations can be divided into three major linguistic and geographic groups: Lakota (Teton, West Dakota), Nakota (Yankton, Central Dakota), and Dakota (Santee, Eastern Dakota).

"The following is the imperfect record of my boyish impressions and experiences up to the age of fifteen years. I have put together these fragmentary recollections of my thrilling wild life expressly for my little son who was born too late to see for himself the drama of such an existence. I dedicate this little book, with love, to Ohiyesa the second, my son."
—Charles A. Eastman (Ohiyesa), Santee Dakota

What boy would not be an Indian for a
while when he thinks of the freest life in the
world? This life was mine. Every day there
was a real hunt. There was real game.

My beautiful mother died soon after I was born. Upon her deathbed she held me close while she whispered to my grandmother. She said, "I give you this boy for your own."

My grandmother was the wisest of guides and the best of protectors. She made all my clothes and my tiny moccasins with a great deal of taste. Sometimes, when I wakened too early, my grandmother would sing me a lullaby.

As a babe I was placed in a movable cradle made from an oak board. In this upright cradle I lived, played, and slept most of the time.

I was capable of conversing in an unknown language with birds and red squirrels. It was common for birds to land on my cradle in the woods.

I was four years old when white men came with their big guns to drive us away from our beautiful country.

The soldiers pursued our people across the Missouri river. We had to cross this dangerous river in buffalo-skin boats—as round as tubs!

When I was six, my father and my two older brothers were taken prisoner by the United States Army. We believed that they had been killed by the whites. I was taught that I must avenge their deaths as soon as I was able to go upon the war-path.

Our wanderings offered us many pleasant experiences but also many hardships and misfortunes. We once had nothing to eat for several days. I remember the six small birds which made up the breakfast for six families one morning. Then we had no dinner or supper to follow!

Soon after this, we came into a region with many buffaloes. Hunger and scarcity were forgotten. Such was the Indian's wild life!

The Indian boy was a prince of the wilderness.
We had very little work. We shot the bow and arrow,
raced our ponies, wrestled, and swam. We played
lacrosse, made war on bees, and sled down hills on
the ribs of animals during the winter.

Every boy was trained to find new and strange things in the woods. If a bird had scratched the leaves off the ground, we stopped to speculate on the time it was done.

An old deer-track brought a discussion as to whether it was a buck or a doe. Every hunt combined the study of animal life. We often marveled at the many beauties and forces of nature.

The Indian boy was a good listener, with a good memory. Very early he began to learn and pass on the legends of his people. Almost every evening a story of some deed done in the past was told by one of the elders. On the following evening I had to repeat the story to the rest of the family.

We also often imitated the customs and habits of our fathers. Occasionally we held a medicine dance off in the woods. We pretended to act like our elders. We painted and imitated our fathers and grandfathers to the smallest detail.

Oesedah was my beautiful little cousin. She was four years younger than me and lived with us for a portion of the year. When I was not in the woods, Oesedah was my companion at home. When I returned from my play at evening, she would have a hundred questions ready for me.

We had many curious wild pets. There were
young foxes, wolves, raccoons, and fawns. There
were also buffalo calves and birds of all kinds.
Oesedah had a pet squirrel which she loved
dearly. I once had a grizzly bear for a pet. So far
as he and I were concerned, our relations were
charming and very close.

Our family was once very short of food in the winter time. As soon as we began to save our food, Oesedah gave some of hers to her beloved pet squirrel. When we were near to starving my grandmother suggested the squirrel be killed for food. But my little cousin cried and held on to it. She said: "Why can't we all die of hunger?" Fortunately, relief came in time to save her pet.

My grandmother was a medicine woman. Once she took me with her into the woods in search of medicinal roots. She explained: "The Great Mystery does not will us to find things too easily. Ohiyesa must learn that there are many secrets. The Great Mystery will tell them only to the most worthy." She said these things so impressively that I can remember them even today.

When I was about five or six, my grandmother turned me over to my uncle, White Footprint, for manly training. He taught me how to hunt for food and to fight in war. He was a strict but good teacher.

In warfare, a young man must be able to go without food and water for two or three days. He must be able to run for a day and a night without any rest. Or he must be able to cross a wild country without losing his way.

Sometimes my uncle would challenge me to go without any food all day long. I had to accept the challenge. We blackened our faces with charcoal, so that every boy in the village would know that I was fasting for the day.

My uncle would also shoot off his rifle just outside of the lodge while I was still asleep, at the same time giving blood-curdling yells.

He expected me to jump up. I should always be ready to grasp a weapon and to give a shrill whoop in reply. After a time, I became used to this.

I have already told how my father was captured by the soldiers. So it may be imagined how I felt toward the Big Knives, as we called the soldiers! On the other hand, I had heard marvelous things of this people. In some things we despised them, and in others we regarded them as mysterious.

When I was told that the Big Knives had created a "fire-boat-walks-on-mountains" (a train) it was too much to believe. Those who saw this monster move said that it flew from mountain to mountain. I confess that the story almost caused me to lose my bravery.

I was now fifteen years old, and was about to enter into a man's life. Then, suddenly, a great change came.

One fine morning my grandmother met me as I returned from the daily hunt. She said: "Your father has come—he whom we thought dead at the hands of the soldiers. He was pardoned by President Lincoln."

After a few days my father and I left the deep woods for the towns of civilization. I felt as if I were dead and traveling to the Spirit Land. Now my life was to be entirely different from the past. Still, I was eager to see some of the wonderful inventions of the white people. When we reached the first town, I gazed with amazement.

Late in the fall we reached the town where my father and some others lived. Here my wild life came to an end, and my school days began. Such are my memories of an Indian boyhood. It is a life that is gone forever. Yet, I repeat, what boy would not be an Indian for a while when he thinks of the freest life in the world?

Notes on the Illustrations

Page 12: This scene shows the inside of the buffalo skin tipi in which Eastman was born. The vertical designs on the background are on the liner inside the tipi, which was often painted. The long bag hanging on the liner behind Eastman's grandmother is a pipe bag used to store a sacred pipe. Eastman's mother is lying against the backrest made of willows held together by leather straps and supported against a tripod of small pine poles. The ground is covered by a buffalo robe.

Pages 14-15: Cradleboards are traditional protective baby-carriers used by many indigenous peoples throughout North America. The many styles reflect the diverse tribal cultures. Cradleboards are built with a protective frame for the infant's spine, in this case an oak board. A rounded cover of deer skin arcs out from the cradleboard to provide shade and head protection for the infant. The deer skin cover is stiffened with beadwork decorated in patterns typical of both the Sioux and Cheyenne tribes, who were close allies. The inside of the cradleboard is padded with a lining of fresh plant fibers, such as moss, cattail down, or shredded bark. The plants have antiseptic properties that nurture healthy skin and serve as a disposable diaper.

Pages 16-17: This illustration of the river crossing in buffalo skin boats is loosely modeled after an 1832 painting by Karl Bodmer. The frameworks of woven saplings, often willows, are covered by the skin of a buffalo bull, hence the name "bull boats." The boats are about four feet in diameter. The hair was often left on the hide to prevent the boats from spinning in the water as they are paddled.

Pages 18-19: The animal that we call the "buffalo" is technically an "American bison". The buffalo were the most important source of food and shelter for all plains Indians. Every part of the animal was used in one or another aspect of their daily life and material culture.

Page 20: Children living on the Great Plains often made sleds out of the ribs of buffalo or elk, which were tied together by rawhide leather.

Pages 22-23: Not all tipis were painted, but the painted tipis shown on these pages and elsewhere in the book show some of the simpler designs that were often used. Many designs have sacred meanings to the owner and were handed down from generation to generation.

Pages 24-25: This scene shows young boys surrounding a sacred tree. The Sioux Sun Dance also has a sacred tree at the center of the Sun Dance Lodge.

Page 26: The design on the back of the tipi is called a "feathered sun." It represents the created universe.

Pages 28-29: Women owned the tipis. Young girls often had small tipis of their own in which they could imitate their mothers.

Pages 32-33: Native peoples first discovered the medicinal properties of indigenous herbs and plants, many of which are still used today.

Pages 42-43: We close this chapter of Eastman's life with an imaginative image of Eastman as warrior mounted on horseback and adorned by an eagle feather headdress. This is set against the background of the feathered sun, representing all of creation. It has been used to symbolize the native spirit of all American Indian people.

These books contain more information about the life of Charles Eastman, including photographs: *The Essential Charles Eastman (Ohiyesa)*, edited by Michael Oren Fitzgerald. World Wisdom, 2007; *Living in Two Worlds*, by Charles Eastman (Ohiyesa), edited by Michael Oren Fitzgerald. World Wisdom, 2010.

ABOUT CHARLES EASTMAN

Charles Eastman (Ohiyesa) was born in a buffalo hide tipi in 1858 in western Minnesota. His father, Tawakanhdeota (Many Lightnings), was Santee Dakota. His mother, Wakantankawin, (Great Spirit Woman), was the daughter of Wak inajin win (Stands Sacred), a Mdewakanton Dakota, and a well-known army officer, Captain Seth Eastman. She was also the granddaughter of Wichasta (Cloud Man), a Mdewakanton Dakota chief.

Charles Eastman was raised in a traditional way of life of the Santee Dakota that existed before Europeans came to this continent. His contributions to our understanding of the American Indian culture are so significant that at the 1933 Chicago World's Fair Eastman was presented a special medal honoring the most distinguished achievements by an American Indian.

Eastman thought his father had been killed by the U.S. Government in the so-called "Sioux Uprising of 1862." In fact, his father had been pardoned by President Lincoln and in 1873 returned to bring his fifteen-year-old son to live in the civilized world of his day.

Eastman went on to receive his undergraduate degree from Dartmouth and his medical degree at Boston College. His first position was on the Pine Ridge Reservation in South Dakota as the government physician for the Lakota Sioux tribe. Dr. Eastman was at Pine Ridge before, during, and after the "Ghost Dance" rebellion of 1890-91, and he cared for the wounded Indians after the massacre at Wounded Knee. In 1893 he accepted a position as field secretary for the YMCA, and for three years traveled extensively throughout the United States and Canada visiting many Indian reservations in an attempt to start new YMCA's in those areas.

In 1897 and '98 Dr. Eastman lived in Washington D.C. as the legal representative and lobbyist for the Sioux tribe. During these years he met leaders from tribes around the country. In 1910 Eastman began his long association with the Boy Scouts, helping Ernest Thompson Seton establish the organization based in large part on the prototype of the American Indian. It was also at about this time that he started to become in high demand as a lecturer and public speaker, traveling extensively in the U.S. and abroad.

Charles Eastman was the first great American Indian author, publishing the first of his eleven books in 1902. Throughout his adult life, he worked tirelessly to improve the conditions on Indian reservations in the hope that they could become strongholds of tribal traditions—in effect cultural homelands. He believed all "First Americans" could live between two worlds, so to speak, by successfully assimilating the best aspects of our modern civilization while rejecting those features that are inconsistent with Christian and traditional native teachings.

In 1928 Ohiyesa purchased land on the north shore of Lake Huron, in Ontario, Canada. For the remainder of his life, in addition to lecturing occasionally, he lived in his remote and primitive cabin in communion with the virgin nature that he loved so dearly. He died in 1939, at the age of eighty.